FRANCIS

The People's Pope

FRANCIS
The People's Pope

Edited by
Vincenzo Sansonetti

RIZZOLI
NEW YORK

New York · Paris · London · Milan

Words of Joy and Hope

by Vincenzo Sansonetti

"And now, we take up this journey," Pope Francis said just after his election, on the evening of March 13, 2013, "a journey of fraternity, of love, of trust among us." Some months have passed since those first surprising steps of Pope Bergoglio, whom his "brother cardinals" went to "the ends of the earth to get." He is no longer a stranger to us: he is with us, one of us. Familiar to us now are his smile, his courteous and jovial nature, his simplicity and sobriety, his inexhaustible capacity for hospitality, united with wise and solid doctrine. "God's face is the face of a merciful father who is always patient," he said on March 17, 2013, at his first *Angelus*. And five days later, speaking to the diplomatic corps, "It is not possible to establish true links with God, while ignoring other people." His attention to those who are poor, who live in pain, who are alone and his constant invitations to look to the "outskirts of existence" reached their historic culmination in his visit to Lampedusa on July 8, 2013. Here, at the Mass, he spoke of a "globalization of indifference" because "we have become used to the suffering of others." And at the Ecclesial Convention of the Diocese of Rome on June 17, 2013, he reminded participants that "true revolution, the revolution that radically transforms life, was brought about by Jesus Christ through his Resurrection."

Not a day passes without one of his words or gestures shaking us and moving us to reflect deeply on our lives. He loves verbs like build, share, serve ("authentic power is service"), forgive, protect ("be protectors of God's gifts!"), and heal, and nouns like freedom, peace, hope ("please do not let yourselves be robbed of hope"), mercy, tenderness ("not the virtue of the weak"), joy ("do not be men and women of sadness"), and solidarity ("a key word of which we must not be frightened"). He draws on everyday expressions, and thus ours is not "an indefinite God dispersed in the air like a spray"; "we think that going to confession is like using a laundromat for sin removal"; life is not "a motor-way with no obstacles." He corrects: priests should be "pastors, not functionaries." Specifies: "Apart from the Church it is not possible to find Jesus." Clarifies: "Faith is not a light that scatters all our darkness, but a lamp that guides our steps in the night and suffices for the journey." Motivates: "Set your stakes on great ideals, the ideals that enlarge the heart." Expresses indignation: "Rampant capitalism has taught the logic of profit at all costs." Defends the dignity of human life: "Human life, the person, are no longer seen as a primary value to be respected and safeguarded, especially if they are poor or disabled, if they are not yet useful—like the unborn child—or are no longer of any use—like the elderly person." Warns: "The Devil is acting," but "God is stronger!" Reassures: "The world is no worse than it was five centuries ago!"

In the memorable Pentecost vigil with the Movements and Associations on May 18, 2013, in front of two hundred thousand people, he explained his roots. "I had the great blessing of growing up in a family in which faith was lived in a simple, practical way," he said. "However, it was my paternal grandmother in particular who influenced my journey of faith." A few days after the election he said, "As you know, my family is of Italian origin," which explains his constant lively "dialogue between places and cultures a great distance apart." The first Jesuit Pope, the first Pope from the Americas, the first Pope to call himself Francis, after the saint of Assisi, Jorge Mario Bergoglio was born on December 17, 1936, the oldest of five brothers, in Buenos Aires, the Argentinean capital, to parents whose origins were in the Piedmont region of Italy. He studied and earned his high school degree as a chemical technician, and did various jobs until he felt his calling to priesthood and in 1958 decided to enter the Society of Jesus. In 1963 he graduated with a degree in philosophy. On December 13, 1969, he was ordained to priesthood at the age of thirty-three. He earned a second degree in theology. He was provincial superior of the Jesuits in Argentina until 1979, and in the 1980s he was rector of the faculty of theology and philosophy at San Miguel, where he was also responsible for a parish. On May 20, 1992, John Paul II nominated him auxiliary bishop of Buenos Aires, of which he became titular archbishop on February 28, 1998. Wojtyła created him cardinal on February 21, 2001. He has a sober and rigorous, almost ascetical, lifestyle, and is always ready to share in the difficulties and needs of the people, who love and respect him. Considered in the 2005 Conclave as Ratzinger's "progressive" challenger, and supported by Cardinal Martini (but deeming himself unready, he himself asked that his votes be given to the German cardinal), he sides with the poor and the persecuted, and criticizes of affluent society and the great financial powers. But his positions on doctrine and ethics hew rigorously to tradition. On March 13, 2013, the second day of the Conclave, he was elected the 265th successor of Saint Peter.

Vanity Fair magazine elected him "man of the year" well ahead of time, partly because of the decisive way he initiated radical reforms and changes in the Curia. *Time* magazine named him the people's pope. On July 28, 2013, speaking with journalists on his way back from the World Youth Day in Brazil, he confessed, "I need people, I need to meet people, to talk to people." But what counts more is that to the faithful of five continents, and to all people of good will, Francis offers courageous words and precious teachings. In homilies, speeches, and greetings, and on other occasions, he reminds us who we are, what our destiny is, what it means to be with Jesus, and how to live our earthly days to the fullest as we await eternal glory. These concepts are hardly new in the two thousand year–history of the Church, but are expressed with a power and candor that strike straight to the heart. With no claim to exhaustively cover the Pope's teachings, in the following pages we present a broad sampling of quotations distilled from Bergoglio's already rich offerings, in chronological order and with our own titles. These are useful reflections in times when sure orientations are scarce. They are accompanied by the most beautiful and meaningful images from the first months of his pontificate.

July 31, 2013
(liturgical feast of Saint Ignatius of Loyola)

———

Journey

And now, we take up this journey: Bishop and People. This journey of the Church of Rome, which presides in charity over all the Churches. A journey of fraternity, of love, of trust among us. Let us always pray for one another. Let us pray for the whole world, that there may be a great spirit of fraternity.

First Apostolic Blessing Urbi et Orbi, *March 13, 2013*

Sand

We can walk as much as we want, we can build many things, but if we do not profess Jesus Christ, things go wrong. We may become a charitable NGO, but not the Church, the Bride of the Lord. When we are not walking, we stop moving. When we are not building on the stones, what happens? The same thing that happens to children on the beach when they build sand castles: Everything is swept away. There is no solidity.

Homily of the Missa Pro Ecclesia, *with the Cardinal Electors, Sistine Chapel, March 14, 2013*

Devil

When we do not profess Jesus Christ, the saying of Léon Bloy comes to mind: "Anyone who does not pray to the Lord prays to the devil." When we do not profess Jesus Christ, we profess the worldliness of the devil, a demonic worldliness.

Homily of the Missa Pro Ecclesia, *with the Cardinal Electors,*
Sistine Chapel, March 14, 2013

Brothers

Inspired by a profound sense of responsibility and supported by a great love for Christ and for the Church, we have prayed together, fraternally sharing our feelings, our experiences, and our reflections. In this atmosphere of great warmth we have come to know one another better in a climate of mutual openness, and this is good, because we are brothers. Someone said to me the Cardinals are the priests of the Holy Father. That community, that friendship, that closeness will do us all good. And our acquaintance and mutual openness have helped us to be docile to the action of the Holy Spirit.

Address to the College of Cardinals, Clementine Hall, March 15, 2013

Service

I express my desire to serve the Gospel with renewed love, helping the Church to become increasingly, in Christ and with Christ, the fruitful vine of the Lord.

Address to the College of Cardinals, Clementine Hall, March 15, 2013

Old Age

Half of us are advanced in age. Old age is—as I like to say—the seat of life's wisdom. The old have acquired the wisdom that comes from having journeyed through life, like the old man Simeon, the old prophetess Anna in the Temple. And that wisdom enabled them to recognize Jesus. Let us pass on this wisdom to the young: like good wine that improves with age, let us give life's wisdom to the young.

Address to the College of Cardinals, Clementine Hall, March 15, 2013

Christ

Christ is the Church's Pastor, but his presence in history passes through the freedom of human beings; from their midst one is chosen to serve as his Vicar, the Successor of the Apostle Peter. Yet Christ remains the center, not the Successor of Peter: Christ, Christ is the center. Christ is the fundamental point of reference, the heart of the Church. Without him, Peter and the Church would not exist or have reason to exist. As Benedict XVI frequently reminded us, Christ is present in Church and guides her.

Audience to Representatives of the Communications Media,
Paul VI Audience Hall, March 16, 2013

Forgiveness

The Lord never tires of forgiving: never! It is we who tire of asking his forgiveness. Let us ask for the grace not to tire of asking forgiveness, because he never tires of forgiving. Let us ask for this grace.

Homily of the Mass in St. Anna, Vatican, March 17, 2013

Patience

God's face is the face of a merciful father who is always patient. Have you thought about God's patience, the patience he has with each one of us? That is his mercy. He always has patience, patience with us, he understands us, he waits for us, he does not tire of forgiving us if we are able to return to him with a contrite heart.

Angelus, *St. Peter's Square, March 17, 2013*

Faithfulness

God does not want a house built by men, but faithfulness to his word, to his plan. It is God himself who builds the house, but from living stones sealed by his Spirit.

Homily of the Mass for the Beginning of the Petrine Ministry,
St. Peter's Square, March 19, 2013

Protecting

The vocation of being a "protector," however, is not just something involving us Christians alone; it also has a prior dimension, which is simply human, involving everyone. It means protecting all creation, the beauty of the created world, as the Book of Genesis tells us and as St. Francis of Assisi showed us. It means respecting each of God's creatures and respecting the environment in which we live. It means protecting people, showing loving concern for each and every person, especially children, the elderly, and those in need, who are often the last we think about. It means caring for one another in our families: husbands and wives first protect one another, and then, as parents, they care for their children, and children themselves, in time, protect their parents.

Homily of the Mass for the Beginning of the Petrine Ministry,
St. Peter's Square, March 19, 2013

Heart

To be "protectors," we also have to keep watch over ourselves! Let us not forget that hatred, envy, and pride defile our lives! Being protectors, then, also means keeping watch over our emotions, over our hearts, because they are the seat of good and evil intentions—intentions that build up and tear down!

Homily of the Mass for the Beginning of the Petrine Ministry,
St. Peter's Square, March 19, 2013

Tenderness

Caring, protecting, demands goodness; it calls for a certain tenderness. In the Gospels, St. Joseph appears as a strong and courageous man, a working man, yet in his heart we see great tenderness, which is not the virtue of the weak but rather a sign of strength of spirit and a capacity for concern, for compassion, for genuine openness to others, for love. We must not be afraid of goodness, of tenderness!

Homily of the Mass for the Beginning of the Petrine Ministry,
St. Peter's Square, March 19, 2013

Power

Let us never forget that authentic power is service, and that the Pope, too, when exercising power, must enter ever more fully into that service, which has its radiant culmination on the Cross. He must be inspired by the lowly, concrete, and faithful service that marked St. Joseph and, like him, he must open his arms to protect all of God's people and embrace with tender affection the whole of humanity, especially the poorest, the weakest, the least important.

Homily of the Mass for the Beginning of the Petrine Ministry,
St. Peter's Square, March 19, 2013

Ecumenism

Dear brothers and sisters in Christ, let us all feel closely united to the prayer of our Saviour at the Last Supper, to his appeal: *ut unum sint.* Let us ask the Father of mercies to enable us to live fully the faith graciously bestowed upon us on the day of our Baptism and to bear witness to it freely, joyfully, and courageously. This will be the best service we can offer to the cause of Christian unity, a service of hope for a world still torn by divisions, conflicts, and rivalries. The more we are faithful to his will—in our thoughts, words, and actions—the more we will progress, really and substantially, toward unity.

Audience with Representatives of the Churches and Ecclesial Communities and of the Different Religions, Clementine Hall, March 20, 2013

Poverty

How many poor people there still are in the world! And what great suffering they have to endure! After the example of Francis of Assisi, the Church in every corner of the globe has always tried to care for and look after those who suffer from want, and I think that in many of your countries you can attest to the generous activity of Christians who dedicate themselves to helping the sick, orphans, the homeless, and all the marginalized, thus striving to make society more humane and more just. But there is another form of poverty! It is the spiritual poverty of our time, which afflicts the so-called richer countries particularly seriously.

To the Diplomatic Corps Accredited to the Holy See,
Apostolic Palace, March 22, 2013

Peace

There is no true peace without truth! There cannot be true peace if everyone is his own criterion, if everyone can always claim exclusively his own rights, without at the same time caring for the good of others, of everyone, on the basis of the nature that unites every human being on this earth.

To the Diplomatic Corps Accredited to the Holy See,
Apostolic Palace, March 22, 2013

Bridges

One of the titles of the Bishop of Rome is Pontiff; that is, a builder of bridges with God, and between people. My wish is that the dialogue between us should help to build bridges connecting all people, in such a way that everyone can see in the other not an enemy, not a rival, but a brother or sister to be welcomed and embraced! My own origins impel me to work for the building of bridges. As you know, my family is of Italian origin; and so this dialogue between places and cultures a great distance apart matters greatly to me—this dialogue between one end of the world and the other, which today are growing ever closer, more interdependent, more in need of opportunities to meet and to create real spaces of authentic fraternity.

To the Diplomatic Corps Accredited to the Holy See,
Apostolic Palace, March 22, 2013

Islam

It is not possible to establish true links with God while ignoring other people. Hence, it is important to intensify dialogue among the various religions, and I am thinking particularly of dialogue with Islam. At the Mass marking the beginning of my ministry, I greatly appreciated the presence of so many civil and religious leaders from the Islamic world. And it is also important to intensify outreach to non-believers, so that the differences that divide and hurt us may never prevail, but rather the desire to build true links of friendship between all peoples, despite their diversity.

To the Diplomatic Corps Accredited to the Holy See,
Apostolic Palace, March 22, 2013

Mercy

Jesus has awakened great hopes, especially in the hearts of the simple, the humble, the poor, the forgotten, those who do not matter in the eyes of the world. He understands human sufferings, he has shown the face of God's mercy, and he has bent down to heal body and soul. This is Jesus. This is his heart, which looks to all of us, to our sicknesses, to our sins. The love of Jesus is great. . . . He is our friend, our brother.

Homily of the Celebration of Palm Sunday of the Passion of Our Lord,
St. Peter's Square, March 24, 2013

Joy

Here the first word that I wish to say to you: *joy*! Do not be men and women of sadness: a Christian can never be sad! Never give way to discouragement! Ours is not a joy born of having many possessions, but from having encountered a Person, Jesus, in our midst; it is born from knowing that with him we are never alone, even at difficult moments, even when our lives' journey comes up against problems and obstacles that seem insurmountable. . . . He accompanies us and carries us on his shoulders. This is our joy. . . .

Homily of the Celebration of Palm Sunday of the Passion of Our Lord,
St. Peter's Square, March 24, 2013

Hope

Please do not let yourselves be robbed of hope! Do not let hope be stolen! The hope that Jesus gives us.

Homily of the Celebration of Palm Sunday of the Passion of Our Lord,
St. Peter's Square, March 24, 2013

Evil

Jesus takes upon himself the evil, the filth, the sin of the world, including the sin of all of us, and he cleanses it; he cleanses it with his blood, with the mercy and the love of God. Let us look around: how many wounds are inflicted upon humanity by evil? Wars, violence, economic conflicts that hit the weakest, greed for money that you can't take with you and have to leave behind.

Homily of the Celebration of Palm Sunday of the Passion of Our Lord,
St. Peter's Square, March 24, 2013

Apostles

In his earthly mission Jesus walked the roads of the Holy Land; he called twelve simple people to stay with him, to share his journey, and to continue his mission. He chose them from among the people full of faith in God's promises.

First General Audience, St. Peter's Square, March 27, 2013

Companionship

Jesus lived the daily reality of the most ordinary people. He was moved as he faced the crowd that seemed like a flock without a shepherd; he wept before the sorrow that Martha and Mary felt at the death of their brother, Lazarus; he called a publican to be his disciple; he also suffered betrayal by a friend. In him, God has given us the certitude that he is with us, he is among us.

First General Audience, St. Peter's Square, March 27, 2013

Samaritan

God thinks like the Samaritan who did not pass by the unfortunate man, pitying him or looking at him from the other side of the road, but helped him without asking for anything in return; without asking whether he was a Jew, a pagan, or a Samaritan; whether he was rich or poor—he asked for nothing. He went to help him; God is like this. God thinks like the shepherd who lays down his life in order to defend and save his sheep.

First General Audience, St. Peter's Square, March 27, 2013

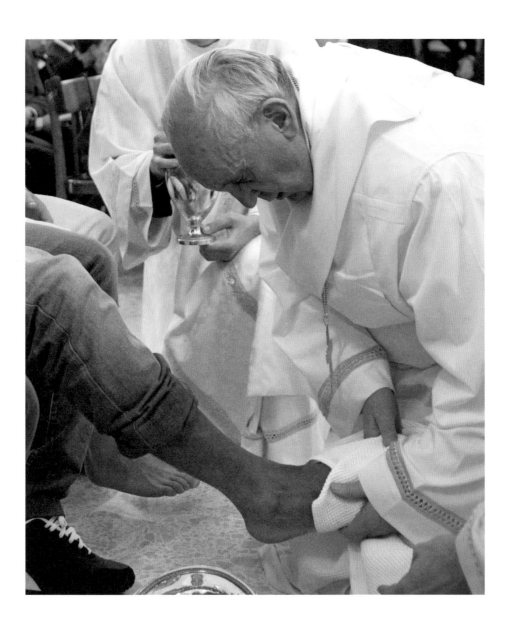

Cross

The Cross is the word through which God has responded to evil in the world. Sometimes it may seem as though God does not react to evil, as if he is silent. And yet, God has spoken, he has replied, and his answer is the Cross of Christ—a word that is love, mercy, forgiveness. It also reveals a judgment, namely that God, in judging us, loves us. Let us remember this: God judges us by loving us. If I embrace his love, then I am saved; if I refuse it, then I am condemned—not by him, but by my own self, because God never condemns, he only loves and saves.

Way of the Cross at the Colosseum, Palantine Hill, March 29, 2013

Surprises

Newness often makes us fearful, including the newness that God brings us, the newness that God asks of us. We are like the Apostles in the Gospel; often we would prefer to hold on to our own security, to stand in front of a tomb, to think about someone who has died, someone who ultimately lives on only as a memory, like the great historical figures from the past. We are afraid of God's surprises. Dear brothers and sisters, we are afraid of God's surprises! He always surprises us! The Lord is like that.

Homily of the Easter Vigil, Vatican Basilica, March 30, 2013

Confidence

Let us not be closed to the newness that God wants to bring into our lives! Are we often weary, disheartened, and sad? Do we feel weighed down by our sins? Do we think that we won't be able to cope? Let us not close our hearts, let us not lose confidence, let us never give up. There are no situations that God cannot change, there is no sin that he cannot forgive if only we open ourselves to him.

Homily of the Easter Vigil, Vatican Basilica, March 30, 2013

Presence

Jesus no longer belongs to the past, but lives in the present and is projected toward the future; Jesus is the everlasting "today" of God. This is how the newness of God appears to the women, the disciples, and all of us: as victory over sin, evil, and death, over everything that crushes life and makes it seem less human. And this is a message meant for me and for you, dear sister; for you, dear brother. How often does Love have to ask us: why do you look for the living among the dead? Our daily problems and worries can wrap us up in ourselves, in sadness and bitterness . . . and that is where death is. That is not the place to look for the One who is alive!

Homily of the Easter Vigil, Vatican Basilica, March 30, 2013

Resurrection

What does it mean that Jesus is risen? It means that the love of God is stronger than evil and death; it means that the love of God can transform our lives and let those desert places in our hearts bloom. The love of God can do this! . . . Jesus did not return to his former life, to earthly life, but entered into the glorious life of God and he entered there with our humanity, opening us to a future of hope.

Urbi et Orbi *Message, St. Peter's Square, March 31, 2013*

Glory

This is what Easter is: it is the exodus, the passage of human beings from slavery to sin and evil to the freedom of love and goodness. Because God is life, life alone, and we are his glory: the living man.

Urbi et Orbi *Message, St. Peter's Square, March 31, 2013*

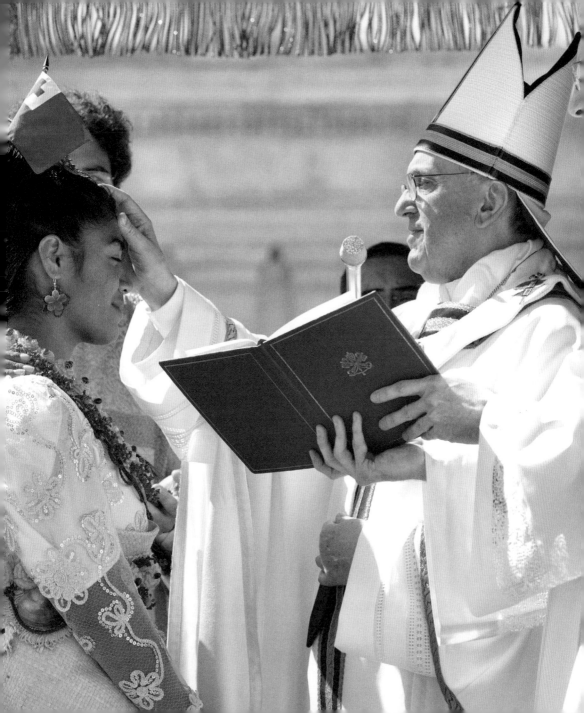

Victory

Easter [is] the central mystery of our faith. May the power of Christ's Resurrection reach every person—especially those who are suffering—and all the situations most in need of trust and hope. Christ has fully triumphed over evil once and for all, but it is up to us, to the people of every epoch, to welcome this victory into our lives and into the actual situations of history and society.

Regina Cæli, St. Peter's Square, April 1, 2013

Grace

The grace contained in the Sacraments of Easter is an enormous potential for the renewal of our personal existence, of family life, of social relations. However, everything passes through the human heart. If I let myself be touched by the grace of the Risen Christ, if I let him change that aspect of mine that is not good, that can hurt me and others, I allow the victory of Christ to be affirmed in my life, to broaden its beneficial action. This is the power of grace! Without grace we can do nothing.

Regina Cæli, St. Peter's Square, April 1, 2013

Happiness

It is the Resurrection itself that opens us to greater hope, for it opens our lives and the life of the world to the eternal future of God, to full happiness, to the certainty that evil, sin, and death may be overcome. And this leads to living daily situations with greater trust, to facing them with courage and determination. Christ's Resurrection illuminates these everyday situations with a new light. The Resurrection of Christ is our strength!

General Audience, St. Peter's Square, April 3, 2013

Women

The first witnesses of the Resurrection were women. And this is beautiful. This is part of the mission of women; of mothers, of women! Witnessing to their children, to their grandchildren, that Jesus is alive, is living, is risen. . . . However, this also makes us think about how women, in the Church and on the journey of faith, had and still have today a special role in opening the doors to the Lord, in following him and in communicating his face, for the gaze of faith is always in need of simple and profound gaze of love.

General Audience, St. Peter's Square, April 3, 2013

Faith

Blessed are those who have not seen but have believed: this is the beatitude of faith! In every epoch and in every place, blessed are those who, on the strength of the word of God proclaimed in the Church and witnessed by Christians, believe that Jesus Christ is the love of God incarnate, Mercy incarnate. And this applies for each one of us!

Regina Cæli, St. Peter's Square, April 7, 2013

Fear

The Spirit of the Risen Christ drove out fear from the Apostles' hearts and impelled them to leave the Upper Room in order to spread the Gospel. Let us too have greater courage in witnessing to our faith in the Risen Christ! We must not be afraid of being Christian and living as Christians! We must have this courage to go and proclaim the Risen Christ, for he is our peace; he made peace with his love, with his forgiveness, with his Blood, and with his mercy.

Regina Cæli, St. Peter's Square, April 7, 2013

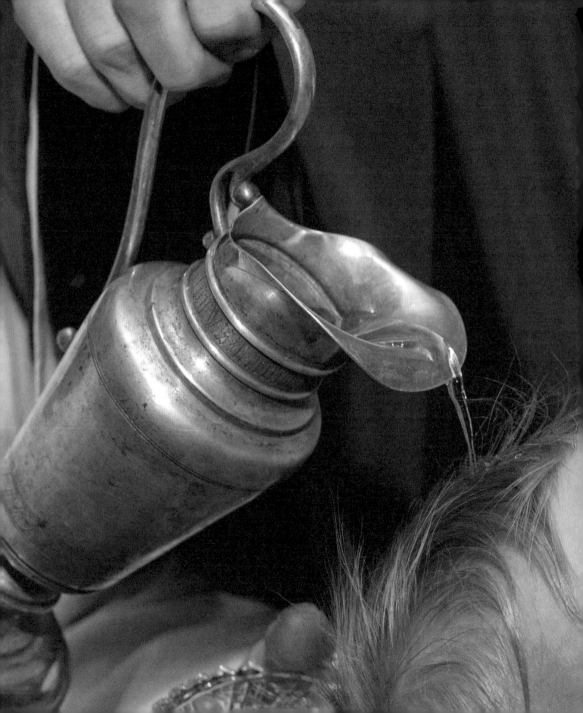

Baptism

With the Resurrection of Jesus, something absolutely new happens: we are set free from the slavery of sin and become children of God; that is, we are born to new life. When is this accomplished for us? In the sacrament of baptism. In ancient times, it was customarily received through immersion. The person who was to be baptized walked down into the great basin of the baptistery, stepping out of his clothes, and the bishop or priest poured water on his head three times, baptizing him in the name of the Father, of the Son, and of the Holy Spirit. Then the baptized person emerged from the basin and put on a new robe, the white one; in other words, by immersing himself in the death and Resurrection of Christ he was born to new life. He had become a son of God.

General Audience, St. Peter's Square, April 10, 2013

Children

We can live as children! And this is our dignity—we have the dignity of children. We should behave as true children! This means that every day we must let Christ transform us and conform us to him; it means striving to live as Christians, endeavoring to follow him in spite of seeing our limitations and weaknesses. The temptation to set God aside in order to put ourselves at the center is always at the door, and the experience of sin injures our Christian life, our being children of God. . . . Only by behaving as children of God, without despairing at our shortcomings, at our sins; only by feeling loved by him will our lives be new, enlivened by serenity and joy.

General Audience, St. Peter's Square, April 10, 2013

Expectations

Hope does not let us down—the hope of the Lord! How often in our lives do hopes vanish, how often do the expectations we have in our heart come to nothing! Our hope as Christians is strong, safe, and sound on this earth, where God has called us to walk, and it is open to eternity because it is founded on God who is always faithful. We must not forget God is always faithful to us.

General Audience, St. Peter's Square, April 10, 2013

Christians

Being Christian is not just obeying orders but means being in Christ, thinking like him, acting like him, loving like him; it means letting him take possession of our lives and change them, transform them and free them from the darkness of evil and sin.

General Audience, St. Peter's Square, April 10, 2013

Word

Our faith is not only centered on a book but on a history of salvation, and, above all, on a Person, Jesus Christ, the Word of God made flesh. Precisely because the horizon of the divine word embraces and extends beyond Scripture, to understand it adequately, the constant presence of the Holy Spirit is necessary.

Address to the Members of the Pontifical Biblical Commission,
Hall of the Popes, April 12, 2013

Persecutions

Apostles were simple people; they were neither scribes nor doctors of the law, nor did they belong to the class of priests. With their limitations and with the authorities against them, how did they manage to fill Jerusalem with their teaching? It is clear that only the presence of the Risen Lord and the action of the Holy Spirit can explain this fact. . . . Their faith was based on such a strong personal experience of the dead and Risen Christ that they feared nothing and no one, and even saw persecution as a cause of honor that enabled them to follow in Jesus's footsteps and to be like him, witnessing with their lives.

Regina Cœli, St. Peter's Square, April 14, 2013

Separation

St. Luke says that having seen Jesus ascending into heaven, the Apostles returned to Jerusalem "with great joy." This seems to us a little odd. When we are separated from our relatives, from our friends, because of a definitive departure and, especially, death, there is usually a natural sadness in us since we will no longer see their faces, no longer hear their voices, or enjoy their love, their presence. The Evangelist instead emphasizes the profound joy of the Apostles. But how could this be? Precisely because, with the gaze of faith, they understand that although he has been removed from their sight, Jesus stays with them forever; he does not abandon them and in the glory of the Father supports them, guides them, and intercedes for them.

General Audience, St. Peter's Square, April 17, 2013

Guide

The Ascension does not point to Jesus's absence, but tells us that he is alive in our midst in a new way. He is no longer in a specific place in the world as he was before the Ascension. He is now in the lordship of God, present in every space and time, close to each one of us. . . . We are never alone; the Crucified and Risen Lord guides us.

General Audience, St. Peter's Square, April 17, 2013

Voice

Jesus wants to establish with his friends a relationship that mirrors his own relationship with the Father: a relationship of reciprocal belonging in full trust, in intimate communion. To express this profound understanding, this friendship, Jesus uses the image of the shepherd with his sheep: he calls them, and they recognize his voice, they respond to his call and follow him. . . . The mystery of his voice is evocative—only think that from our mother's womb we learn to recognize her voice and that of our father; it is from the tone of a voice that we perceive love or contempt, affection or coldness. Jesus's voice is unique! If we learn to distinguish it, he guides us on the path of life, a path that goes beyond even the abyss of death.

Regina Cæli, St. Peter's Square, April 21, 2013

Church

Apart from the Church it is not possible to find Jesus. The great Paul VI said, "It is an absurd dichotomy to wish to live with Jesus but without the Church, to follow Jesus but without the Church, to love Jesus but without the Church."

Homily of the Mass for the Feast of St. George, Pauline Church, April 23, 2013

Consolation

If we want to take the path of worldliness, bargaining with the world . . . we will never have the consolation of the Lord. And if we seek consolation alone, it will be a superficial consolation—not the Lord's consolation, but a human consolation. The Church always advances between the cross and the Resurrection, between persecutions and the consolations of the Lord. This is the path: those who take this path do not go wrong.

Homily of the Mass for the Feast of St. George, Pauline Church, April 23, 2013

Last Judgment

Human history begins with the creation of man and woman in God's likeness and ends with the Last Judgment of Christ. These two poles of history are often forgotten; and, at times, especially faith in Christ's return and in the Last Judgment, they are not so clear and firm in Christian hearts.

General Audience, St. Peter's Square, April 24, 2013

Watchfulness

We do not know either the day or the hour of Christ's return. What he asks of us is to be ready for the encounter . . . which means being able to see the signs of his presence, keeping our faith alive with prayer, with the sacraments, and taking care not to fall asleep so as not to forget about God. The life of slumbering Christians is a sad life; it is not a happy life. Christians must be happy. . . .

General Audience, Pauline Church, April 24, 2013

Talents

In particular, in this period of crisis, today, it is important not to turn in on ourselves, burying our own talents, our spiritual, intellectual, and material riches, everything that the Lord has given us, but rather to open ourselves, to be supportive, to be attentive to others. . . . Do not bury your talents! Set your stakes on great ideals, the ideals that enlarge the heart, the ideals of service that make your talents fruitful. Life is not given to us to be jealously guarded for ourselves, but is given to us so that we may give it in turn.

General Audience, Pauline Church, April 24, 2013

Gift

We must always have clearly in mind that we are justified, we are saved through grace, through an act of freely given love by God who always goes before us; on our own we can do nothing. Faith is, first of all, a gift we have received. But in order to bear fruit, God's grace always demands our openness to him, our free and tangible response. Christ comes to bring us the mercy of a god who saves. We are asked to trust in him, to correspond to the gift of his love with a good life, made up of actions motivated by faith and love.

General Audience, Pauline Church, April 24, 2013

Servants

May looking at the Last Judgment never frighten us; rather, may it impel us to live the present better. God offers us this time with mercy and patience so that we may learn every day to recognize him in the poor and in the lowly. Let us strive for goodness and be watchful in prayer and in love. May the Lord, at the end of our lives and at the end of history, be able to recognize us as good and faithful servants.

General Audience, Pauline Church, April 24, 2013

Work

Work is part of God's loving plan; we are called to cultivate and care for all the goods of creation and in this way share in the work of creation! Work is fundamental to the dignity of a person. . . . It gives one the ability to maintain oneself and one's family, to contribute to the growth of one's own nation. And here I think of the difficulties that, in various countries, today afflict the world of work and business; I am thinking of how many—and not only young people—are unemployed, often due to a purely economic conception of society, which selfishly seeks profit beyond the parameters of social justice.

General Audience, St. Peter's Square, May 1, 2013

Future

I would like to speak especially to you, young people: be committed to your daily duties, your studies, your work, to friendships, to helping others. Your future also depends on how you live these precious years of your life. Do not be afraid of commitment, of sacrifice, and do not view the future with fear. Keep your hope alive: there is always a light on the horizon.

General Audience, St. Peter's Square, May 1, 2013

Prayer

To listen to the Lord, we must learn to contemplate, feel his constant presence in our lives, and we must stop and converse with him, give him space in prayer. Each of us . . . should ask ourselves, "How much space do I give to the Lord? Do I stop to talk with him?" Ever since we were children, our parents have taught us to start and end the day with a prayer, to teach us to feel that the friendship and the love of God accompanies us. . . . Praying together is a precious moment that further strengthens family life, friendship! Let us learn to pray more in the family and as a family!

General Audience, St. Peter's Square, May 1, 2013

Mother

Mary is the mother, and a mother worries above all about the health of her children; she knows how to care for them always with great and tender love. Our Lady guards our health. What does this mean— "Our Lady guards our health"? I think, above all, of three things: she helps us grow, to confront life, to be free.

Recital of the Holy Rosary, Papal Basilica of St. Mary Major, May 4, 2013

Education

You do not teach, you do not take care of health by avoiding problems, as though life were a motorway with no obstacles. The mother helps her children to see the problems of life realistically and not to get lost in them, but to confront them with courage, not to be weak, and to know how to overcome them, in a healthy balance that a mother "senses" between the area of security and the area of risk. And a mother can do this! She does not always take the child along the safe road, because in that way the child cannot develop, but neither does she leave the child only on the risky path, because that is dangerous. A mother knows how to balance things. A life without challenges does not exist, and a boy or a girl who cannot face or tackle them is a boy or girl with no backbone!

Recital of the Holy Rosary, Papal Basilica of St. Mary Major, May 4, 2013

Freedom

What does freedom mean? It is certainly not doing whatever you want, allowing yourself to be dominated by the passions, to pass from one experience to another without discernment, to follow the fashions of the day; freedom does not mean, so to speak, throwing everything that you don't like out the window. No, that is not freedom! Freedom is given to us so that we know how to make good decisions in life! Mary, as a good mother, teaches us to be, like her, capable of making definitive decisions; definitive choices, at this moment, in a time controlled by, so to speak, a philosophy of the provisional. It is very difficult to make a lifetime commitment. And she helps us to make those definitive decisions in the full freedom with which she said yes to the plan God had for her life.

Recital of the Holy Rosary, Papal Basilica of St. Mary Major, May 4, 2013

Provisional

How difficult it is to take a final decision in our time. Temporary things seduce us. We are victims of a trend that pushes us to the provisional . . . as though we wanted to stay adolescents. There is a little charm in staying adolescents, and this for life! Let us not be afraid of life commitments, commitments that take up and concern our entire lives! In this way our lives will be fruitful! And this is freedom: to have the courage to make these decisions with generosity.

Recital of the Holy Rosary, Papal Basilica of St. Mary Major, May 4, 2013

Chastity

Chastity for the Kingdom of Heaven shows how the emotions have their place in mature freedom and become a sign of the world to come, to make God's primacy shine out ever brighter. But, please, let it be a "fruitful" chastity, which generates spiritual children in the Church. The consecrated woman is a mother; she must be a mother, not a "spinster"! Excuse me for speaking like this, but motherhood in the consecrated life is important, this fruitfulness! May this joy of spiritual fecundity motivate your life; be mothers, as a figure of Mary, Mother, and of Mother Church. It is impossible to understand Mary without her motherhood; it is impossible to understand the Church apart from her motherhood, and you are icons of Mary and the Church.

Address to the Plenary Assembly of the International Union of Superiors General, Paul VI Audience Hall, May 8, 2013

Living Water

The Holy Spirit is the inexhaustible source of God's life in us. Man of every time and place desires a full and beautiful life, just and good, a life that is not threatened by death, but can still mature and grow to fullness. Man is like a traveler who, crossing the deserts of life, thirsts for the living water: gushing and fresh, capable of quenching his deep desire for light, love, beauty, and peace. We all feel this desire! And Jesus gives us this living water: he is the Holy Spirit, who proceeds from the Father and whom Jesus pours out into our hearts.

General Audience, St. Peter's Square, May 8, 2013

Perception

This is the precious gift that the Holy Spirit brings to our hearts: the very life of God; the life of true children; a relationship of confidence, freedom, and trust in the love and mercy of God. It also gives us a new perception of others, close and far, seen always as brothers and sisters in Jesus to be respected and loved. The Holy Spirit teaches us to see with the eyes of Christ, to live life as Christ lived, to understand life as Christ understood it.

General Audience, St. Peter's Square, May 8, 2013

Truth

Does "the" truth really exist? What is "the" truth? Can we know it? Can we find it? Here springs to my mind the question of Pontius Pilate, the Roman Procurator, when Jesus reveals to him the deep meaning of his mission: "What is truth?" . . . Pilate cannot understand that "the" Truth is standing in front of him, he cannot see in Jesus the face of the truth that is the face of God. And yet Jesus is exactly this: the Truth that, in the fullness of time, "became flesh" . . . and came to dwell among us so that we might know it. The truth is not grasped as a thing—the truth is encountered. It is not a possession—it is an encounter with a Person.

General Audience, St. Peter's Square, May 15, 2013

Grandmother

I had the great blessing of growing up in a family in which faith was lived in a simple, practical way. However, it was my paternal grandmother, in particular, who influenced my journey of faith. She was a woman who explained to us, who talked to us about Jesus, who taught us the Catechism. I always remember that on the evening of Good Friday, she would take us to the candlelight procession, and at the end of this procession "the dead Christ" would arrive and our grandmother would make us—the children—kneel down and she would say to us, "Look, he is dead, but tomorrow he will rise." This was how I received my first Christian proclamation, from this very woman, from my grandmother!

Vigil of Pentecost, with the Ecclesial Movements, St. Peter's Square, May 18, 2013

Calling

The truth is that someone was waiting for me. He had been waiting for me for some time. After making my confession I felt something had changed. I was not the same. I had heard something like a voice, or a call. I was convinced that I should become a priest. This experience of faith is important. We say we must seek God—go to him and ask forgiveness—but when we go, he is waiting for us; he is there first!

Vigil of Pentecost, with the Ecclesial Movements, St. Peter's Square, May 18, 2013

Strength

He understands. I feel great comfort when I think of the Lord looking at me. We think we have to pray and talk, talk, talk. . . . No! Let the Lord look at you. When he looks at us, he gives us strength and helps us to bear witness to him. . . .

Vigil of Pentecost, with the Ecclesial Movements, St. Peter's Square, May 18, 2013

Preaching

The Church is neither a political movement nor a well-organized structure. That is not what she is. We are not an NGO, and when the Church becomes an NGO, she loses her salt, she has no savor; she is only an empty organization. We need cunning here, because the devil deceives us, and we risk falling into the trap of hyperefficiency. Preaching Jesus is one thing; attaining goals, being efficient, is another.

Vigil of Pentecost, with the Ecclesial Movements, St. Peter's Square, May 18, 2013

Outskirts

When the Church is closed, she falls sick, she falls sick. Think of a room that has been closed for a year. When you go into it there is a smell of damp, many things are wrong with it. A Church closed in on herself is the same—a sick Church. The Church must step outside herself. To go where? To the outskirts of existence, whatever they may be. . . .

Vigil of Pentecost, with the Ecclesial Movements, St. Peter's Square, May 18, 2013

Friendship

With our faith we must create a "culture of encounter," a culture of friendship, a culture in which we find brothers and sisters, in which we can also speak with those who think differently, as well as those who hold other beliefs, who do not have the same faith. They all have something in common with us: they are images of God, they are children of God. Going out to meet everyone.

Vigil of Pentecost, with the Ecclesial Movements, St. Peter's Square, May 18, 2013

Witness

There are more martyrs today than there were in the early centuries of the Church. More martyrs! Our own brothers and sisters. They are suffering! They carry their faith even to martyrdom. However, martyrdom is never a defeat; martyrdom is the highest degree of the witness we must give. We are on the way to martyrdom, as small martyrs. . . .

Vigil of Pentecost, with the Ecclesial Movements, St. Peter's Square, May 18, 2013

Newness

Newness always makes us a bit fearful, because we feel more secure if we have everything under control, if we are the ones who build, program, and plan our lives in accordance with our own ideas, our own comfort, our own preferences. This is also the case when it comes to God. Often we follow him, we accept him, but only up to a certain point. It is hard to abandon ourselves to him with complete trust, allowing the Holy Spirit to be the soul and guide of our lives in our every decision. We fear that God may force us to strike out on new paths and leave behind our all too narrow, closed, and selfish horizons in order to become open to his own.

Solemnity of Pentecost Holy Mass, with the Ecclesial Movements,
St. Peter's Square, May 19, 2013

Harmony

When we are the ones who try to create diversity and close ourselves up in what makes us different and other, we bring division. When we are the ones who want to build unity in accordance with our human plans, we end up creating uniformity, standardization. But if instead we let ourselves be guided by the Spirit, [then] richness, variety, and diversity never become a source of conflict, because he impels us to experience variety within the communion of the Church.

Solemnity of Pentecost Holy Mass, with the Ecclesial Movements,
St. Peter's Square, May 19, 2013

Mission

The older theologians used to say that the soul is a kind of sailboat, the Holy Spirit is the wind that fills its sails and drives it forward, and the gusts of wind are the gifts of the Spirit. Lacking his impulse and his grace, we do not go forward. The Holy Spirit draws us into the mystery of the living God and saves us from the threat of a Church that is gnostic and self-referential, closed in on herself; he impels us to open the doors and go forth to proclaim and bear witness to the good news of the Gospel, to communicate the joy of faith, the encounter with Christ. The Holy Spirit is the soul of *mission*.

Solemnity of Pentecost Holy Mass, with the Ecclesial Movements,
St. Peter's Square, May 19, 2013

Home

"Home" is a word with a typically familiar flavor, which recalls warmth, affection, love that can be felt in a family. Hence, the "home" represents the most precious human treasures: that of encounter, that of relations among people—different in age, culture, and history—who live together and help one another to grow. For this reason, the "home" is a crucial place in life, where life grows and can be fulfilled, because it is a place where every person learns to receive love and to give love. This is "home."

Visit at the Dono Di Maria Homeless Shelter, Vatican, May 21, 2013

Loving

To love God and neighbor is not something abstract, but profoundly concrete: it means seeing in every person the face of the Lord to be served, to serve him concretely.

Visit at the Dono Di Maria Homeless Shelter, Vatican, May 21, 2013

Capitalism

We must recover the whole sense of gift, of gratuitousness, of solidarity. Rampant capitalism has taught the logic of profit at all costs, of giving to get, of exploitation without looking at the person . . . and we see the results in the crisis we are experiencing!

Visit at the Dono Di Maria Homeless Shelter, Vatican, May 21, 2013

Communion

The language of the Spirit, the language of the Gospel, is the language of communion, which invites us to get the better of closedness and indifference, division and antagonization. We must all ask ourselves: how do I let myself be guided by the Holy Spirit in such a way that my life and my witness of faith are both unity and communion? Do I convey the word of reconciliation and of love, which is the Gospel, to the milieus in which I live? At times it seems that we are repeating today what happened at Babel: division, the incapacity to understand one another, rivalry, envy, egoism. What do I do with my life? Do I create unity around me? Or do I cause division, by gossip, criticism, or envy? What do I do? Let us think about this.

General Audience, St. Peter's Square, May 22, 2013

Evangelizing

The fire of Pentecost, from the action of the Holy Spirit, releases an ever-new energy for mission, new ways in which to proclaim the message of salvation, new courage for evangelizing. Let us never close ourselves to this action! Let us live the Gospel humbly and courageously! Let us witness to the newness, hope, and joy that the Lord brings to life. . . . Because evangelizing, proclaiming Jesus, gives us joy. Instead, egoism makes us bitter and sad, and depresses us. Evangelizing uplifts us.

General Audience, St. Peter's Square, May 22, 2013

Pastors

Being pastors means believing every day in the grace and strength that come to us from the Lord despite our weakness, and wholly assuming the responsibility for walking *before* the flock, relieved of the burdens that obstruct healthy apostolic promptness, hesitant leadership, so as to make our voices recognizable both to those who have embraced the faith and to those who "are not [yet] of this fold." We are called to make our own the dream of God, whose house knows no exclusion of people or peoples, as Isaiah prophetically foretold. . . .

Profession of Faith with the Bishops of the Italian Episcopal Conference,
Vatican Basilica, May 23, 2013

Money

In a world in which a lot is said about rights, how often is human dignity actually trampled upon! In a world in which so much is said about rights, it seems that the only thing that has any rights is money. Dear brothers and sisters, we are living in a world where money commands. We are living in a world, in a culture, where the fixation on money holds sway.

Address to the Participants in the Plenary of the Pontifical Council for the Pastoral Care of Migrants and Itinerant People, Clementine Hall, May 24, 2013

Love

As [a] Church we should remember that in tending the wounds of refugees, evacuees, and the victims of trafficking, we are putting into practice the commandment of love that Jesus bequeathed to us when he identified with the foreigner, with those who are suffering, with all the innocent victims of violence and exploitation.

Address to the Participants in the Plenary of the Pontifical Council for the Pastoral Care of Migrants and Itinerant People, Clementine Hall, May 24, 2013

Spray

God is not something vague, our God is not a god "spray," he is tangible; he is not abstract but has a name: "God is love." His is not a sentimental, emotional kind of love, but the love of the Father who is the origin of all life, the love of the Son who dies on the Cross and is raised, the love of the Spirit who renews human beings and the world.

Angelus, *St. Peter's Square, May 26, 2013*

Call

The Church is born from God's wish to call all people to communion with him, to friendship with him; indeed, to share in his own divine life as his sons and daughters. The very word "Church," from the Greek *ekklesia*, means "convocation": God convokes us, he impels us to come out of our individualism, from our tendency to close ourselves into ourselves, and he calls us to belong to his family. Furthermore, this call originates in creation itself. God created us so that we might live in a profound friendship with him, and even when sin broke off this relationship with him, with others and with creation, God did not abandon us.

General Audience, St. Peter's Square, May 29, 2013

Shortcomings

Still today some say, "Christ yes, the Church no." Like those who say, "I believe in God but not in priests." But it is the Church herself that brings Christ to us and that brings us to God. The Church is the great family of God's children. Of course, she also has human aspects. In those who make up the Church, pastors and faithful, there are shortcomings, imperfections, and sins. The Pope has these too—and many of them—but what is beautiful is that when we realize we are sinners, we encounter the mercy of God who always forgives. Never forget it: God always pardons.

General Audience, St. Peter's Square, May 29, 2013

Eucharist

It is in listening to his word, in nourishing ourselves with his Body and his Blood that he moves us from being a multitude to being a community, from anonymity to communion. The Eucharist is the sacrament of communion that brings us out of individualism, so that we may follow him together, living out our faith in him. Therefore, we should all ask ourselves before the Lord: how do I live the Eucharist? Do I live it anonymously or as a moment of true communion with the Lord, and also with all the brothers and sisters who share this same banquet? What are our Eucharistic celebrations like?

Holy Mass on the Solemnity of Corpus Christi,
Basilica of St. John Lateran, May 30, 2013

Solidarity

In the Church, but also in society, a key word of which we must not be frightened is "solidarity," that is, the ability to make what we have, our humble capacities, available to God, for only in sharing, in giving, will our lives be fruitful. Solidarity is a word seen negatively by the spirit of the world!

Holy Mass on the Solemnity of Corpus Christi,
Basilica of St. John Lateran, May 30, 2013

Listening

Mary knew how to listen to God. Be careful: it was not merely "hearing," a superficial word, but "listening," which consists of attention, acceptance, and availability to God. It was not in the distracted way with which we sometimes face the Lord or others: we hear their words, but we do not really listen. Mary is attentive to God. She listens to God. However, Mary also listens to the events; that is, she interprets the events of her life, she is attentive to reality itself and does not stop on the surface but goes to the depths to grasp its meaning. . . . This is also true in our lives: listening to God who speaks to us, and listening also to daily reality, paying attention to people, to events, because the Lord is at the door of our lives and knocks in many ways. . . .

Recital of the Holy Rosary for the Conclusion of the Marian Month of May,
St. Peter's Square, May 31, 2013

Decision

It is difficult in life to make decisions. We often tend to put them off, to let others decide instead; we frequently prefer to let ourselves be dragged along by events, to follow the current fashion. At times we know what we ought to do, but we do not have the courage to do it or it seems to us too difficult, because it means swimming against the tide. In the Annunciation, in the Visitation, and at the wedding of Cana, Mary goes against the tide. Mary goes against the tide; she listens to God, she reflects and seeks to understand reality and decides to entrust herself totally to God. Although she is with child, she decides to visit her elderly relative and she decides to entrust herself to her Son with insistence so as to preserve the joy of the wedding feast.

Recital of the Holy Rosary for the Conclusion of the Marian Month of May,
St. Peter's Square, May 31, 2013

Action

We . . . stop at listening, at thinking about what we must do; we may even be clear about the decision we have to make, but we do not move on to action. And, above all, we do not put ourselves at stake by moving toward others "with haste" so as to bring them our help, our understanding, our love; to bring them, like Mary, the most precious thing we have received, Jesus and his Gospel, with words and, above all, with the tangible witness of what we do.

Recital of the Holy Rosary for the Conclusion of the Marian Month of May,
St. Peter's Square, May 31, 2013

Person

Men and women are sacrificed to the idols of profit and consumption: it is the "culture of waste." . . . This "culture of waste" tends to become a common mentality that infects everyone. Human life, the person, are no longer seen as a primary value to be respected and safeguarded, especially if they are poor or disabled, if they are not yet useful—like the unborn child—or are no longer of any use—like the elderly person.

General Audience, St. Peter's Square, June 5, 2013

Against the Tide

Be free people! What do I mean? Perhaps it is thought that freedom means doing everything one likes, or seeing how far one can go by trying drunkenness and overcoming boredom. This is not freedom. Freedom means being able to think about what we do, being able to assess what is good and what is bad; these are the types of conduct that lead to development. It means always opting for the good. Let us be free for goodness. And in this do not be afraid to go against the tide, even if it is not easy! Always being free to choose goodness is demanding, but it will make you into people with a backbone who can face life, people with courage and patience. . . .

Address to the Students of the Jesuit Schools of Italy and Albania,
Paul VI Audience Hall, June 7, 2013

Crisis

Right now the whole world is in crisis. And crisis is not a bad thing. It is true that the crisis causes us suffering, but we—and first and foremost all you young people—must know how to interpret the crisis. What does this crisis mean? What must I do to help us to come through this crisis? The crisis we are experiencing at this time is a human crisis. People say it is an economic crisis, it is a crisis of work. Yes, that's true. But why? This work problem, this problem in the economy, is a consequence of the great human problem. What is in crisis is the value of the human person, and we must defend the human person.

Address to the Students of the Jesuit Schools of Italy and Albania,
Paul VI Audience Hall, June 7, 2013

CAMINAREMO
PAPA FRA
HUMILDE F
NUESTR
BILINGH

People

I would also like to say to anyone who feels far away from God and the Church, to anyone who is timid or indifferent, to those who think they can no longer change: the Lord calls you too to become part of his people, and he does this with great respect and love! He invites us to be part of this people, the People of God! How does one become a member of this people? It is not through physical birth, but through a new birth. In the Gospel, Jesus tells Nicodemus that he needs to be born from on high, from water and from the Spirit in order to enter the Kingdom of God.

General Audience, St. Peter's Square, June 12, 2013

Lord

Look around us—it is enough to open a newspaper . . . we see the presence of evil, the Devil is acting. However, I would like to say out loud: God is stronger! Do you believe this, that God is stronger? Let us say it together, let us say it all together: God is stronger! And do you know why he is stronger? Because he is Lord, the only Lord. And I would like to add that reality, at times dark and marked by evil, can change, if we first bring the light of the Gospel, especially through our lives.

General Audience, St. Peter's Square, June 12, 2013

Dialogue

There are so many human issues to be discussed and shared, and in dialogue it is always possible to come close to the truth, which is a gift of God, and to be mutually enriching. Carrying on a dialogue means being convinced that others have something good to say; it means making room for their viewpoint, their opinion, their suggestions, without, obviously, slipping into relativism. And in order to keep up a dialogue, it is necessary to lower one's guard and open doors. Persevere in the dialogue with cultural, social, and political institutions, in order to make your contribution to the formation of citizens as well, so that they may have at heart the good of all and work for the common good.

Address to the Community of Writers of La Civiltà Cattolica,
Hall of Popes, June 14, 2013

Culture

God is at work in the life of every person and in culture: the Spirit blows where he wills. Endeavor to find out what God has brought about and how to continue his action. . . . And seeking God in all things, in all the fields of knowledge, of art, of science, of political and social life, and of economics requires study, sensitivity, and experience.

Address to the Community of Writers of La Civiltà Cattolica,
Hall of Popes, June 14, 2013

Economy

The goal of economics and politics is to serve humanity, beginning with the poorest and most vulnerable, wherever they may be, even in their mothers' wombs. Every economic and political theory or action must set about providing each inhabitant of the planet with the minimum wherewithal to live in dignity and freedom, with the possibility of supporting a family, educating children, praising God, and developing one's own human potential. This is the main thing; in the absence of such a vision, all economic activity is meaningless.

Letter to H. E. Mr. David Cameron, British Prime Minister,
on the Occasion of the G8 Meeting, June 15, 2013

Life

Jesus is the incarnation of the Living God, the one who brings life amid so many deeds of death, amid sin, selfishness, and self-absorption. Jesus accepts, loves, uplifts, encourages, forgives, restores the ability to walk, gives back life. Throughout the Gospels we see how Jesus, by his words and actions, brings the transforming life of God. This was the experience of the woman who anointed the feet of the Lord with ointment. She felt understood, loved, and she responded by a gesture of love: she let herself be touched by God's mercy, she obtained forgiveness, and she started a new life. God, the Living One, is merciful.

Holy Mass for Evangelium Vitae *Day, St. Peter's Square, June 16, 2013*

Realism

Christians are "spiritual." This does not mean that we are people who live "in the clouds," far removed from real life, as if it were some kind of mirage. No! The Christian is someone who thinks and acts in everyday life according to God's will, someone who allows his or her life to be guided and nourished by the Holy Spirit, to be a full life, a life worthy of true sons and daughters. And this entails realism and fruitfulness. Those who let themselves be led by the Holy Spirit are realists; they know how to survey and assess reality. They are also fruitful; their lives bring new life to birth all around them.

Holy Mass for Evangelium Vitae *Day, St. Peter's Square, June 16, 2013*

Revolution

The revolutions of history have changed political and economic systems, but none have really changed the human heart. True revolution, the revolution that radically transforms life, was brought about by Jesus Christ through his Resurrection.

Address to the Participants in the Ecclesial Convention of the Diocese of Rome,
Paul VI Audience Hall, June 17, 2013

Saints

To become holy we do not need to turn our eyes away and look somewhere else, or have, as it were, the face on a holy card! No, no, that is not necessary. To become saints only one thing is necessary: to accept the grace that the Father gives us in Jesus Christ. There, this grace changes our heart.

Address to the Participants in the Ecclesial Convention of the Diocese of Rome,
Paul VI Audience Hall, June 17, 2013

Walls

Love is the greatest power for the transformation of reality because it pulls down the walls of selfishness and fills the ditches that keep us apart. This is the love that comes from a mutated heart, from a heart of stone that has been turned into a heart of flesh, a human heart. And this is what grace does, the grace of Jesus Christ, which we have all received. . . . Grace is neither bought nor sold; it is a gift of God in Jesus Christ. Jesus Christ gives us grace. He is the only one who gives us grace. It is a present: he is offering it to us, to us. Let us accept it.

Address to the Participants in the Ecclesial Convention of the Diocese of Rome,
Paul VI Audience Hall, June 17, 2013

Sadness

There are people who live without hope. Each one of us can think in silence of people who live with no hope and are steeped in profound sadness from which they struggle to emerge, believing they have found happiness in alcohol, in drugs, in gambling, in the power of money, in sexuality unbridled by rules. . . . However, they find themselves even more disappointed and sometimes vent their rage against life with violent behavior unworthy of the human being. How many sad people, how many sad people. . . .

Address to the Participants in the Ecclesial Convention of the Diocese of Rome,
Paul VI Audience Hall, June 17, 2013

Crossroads

Reaching out to the poor does not mean we must become champions of poverty or, as it were, "spiritual tramps"! No, no, this is not what it means! It means we must reach out to the flesh of Jesus that is suffering, but also suffering is the flesh of Jesus of those who do not know it with their study, with their intelligence, with their culture. We must go there! I, therefore, like using the expression "to go toward the outskirts," the outskirts of existence. All, all the outskirts, from physical and real poverty to intellectual poverty, which is also real. All the peripheries, all the crossroads on the way: go there. And sow there the seed of the Gospel with your words and your witness.

Address to the Participants in the Ecclesial Convention of the Diocese of Rome,
Paul VI Audience Hall, June 17, 2013

Courage

We must have courage. Paul VI used to say that he did not understand disheartened Christians; he simply did not understand those sad and anxious Christians who make one wonder whether they believe in God or in "the goddess of complaint." One never knows. Day in, day out they complain, they moan; see how the world is going, look what disasters, what disasters. But think: the world is no worse than it was five centuries ago! The world is the world; it always was the world. . . . Christians must be brave. In facing a problem, in facing a social or religious crisis, they must have the courage to move onward, to go ahead bravely.

Address to the Participants in the Ecclesial Convention of the Diocese of Rome,
Paul VI Audience Hall, June 17, 2013

Unity

Let us not go down the path of division, of fighting among ourselves! All united, all united in our differences, but united, always: this is the way of Jesus. Unity is superior to conflict. Unity is a grace for which we must ask the Lord that he may liberate us from the temptation of division, of conflict between us, of selfishness, of gossip.

General Audience, St. Peter's Square, June 19, 2013

Justice

The human person and human dignity risk being turned into vague abstractions in the face of issues, like the use of force, war, malnutrition, marginalization, violence, the violation of basic liberties, and financial speculation, which presently affects the price of food, treating it like any other merchandise and overlooking its primary function. Our duty is to continue to insist, in the present international context, that the human person and human dignity are not simply catchwords, but pillars for creating shared rules and structures capable of passing beyond purely pragmatic or technical approaches in order to eliminate divisions and to bridge existing differences.

Address to the Participants in the 38th Conference of Food and Agriculture Organization of the United Nations (FAO), Clementine Hall, June 20, 2013

Sharing

Human beings are not islands; we are a community. My thoughts turn to the well-known parable in the Gospel where a Samaritan helps someone in need. He is not prompted by philanthropy or the fact that he has money at his disposal, but by a desire to identify with the person he helps: he wants to share his lot. Indeed, after providing for the man's care, he announces that he will return to inquire after his health. What is involved here is more than mere compassion or perhaps a desire to share or to promote a reconciliation that can overcome differences and disagreements. It is a willingness to share everything and to decide to be Good Samaritans, instead of people who are indifferent before the needs of others.

Address to the Participants in the 38th Conference of Food and Agriculture Organization of the United Nations (FAO), Clementine Hall, June 20, 2013

Family

Family is the principal setting for the growth of each individual, since it is through the family that human beings become open to life and to the natural need for relationships with others. Over and over again we see that family bonds are essential for the stability of relationships in society, for the work of education, and for integral human development, for they are inspired by love, responsible intergenerational solidarity, and mutual trust. These are factors that can make even the most adverse situations more bearable, and bring a spirit of true fraternity to our world, enabling it to feel as a single family, where the greatest attention is paid to those most in need.

Address to the Participants in the 38th Conference of Food and Agriculture Organization of the United Nations (FAO), Clementine Hall, June 20, 2013

Everyday Life

How many dads and moms every day put their faith into practice by offering up their own lives in a concrete way for the good of the family? Think about this! How many priests, brothers, and sisters carry out their service generously for the Kingdom of God? How many young people renounce their own interests in order to dedicate themselves to children, the disabled, the elderly. . . . They are martyrs too! Daily martyrs, martyrs of everyday life! And then there are many people, Christians and non-Christians alike, who "lose their lives" for truth. And Christ said, "I am the truth," therefore, whoever serves the truth serves Christ.

Angelus, *St. Peter's Square, June 23, 2013*

Lamp

Faith is not a light that scatters all our darkness, but a lamp that guides our steps in the night and suffices for the journey. To those who suffer, God does not provide arguments that explain everything; rather, his response is that of an accompanying presence, a history of goodness, which touches every story of suffering and opens up a ray of light. In Christ, God himself wishes to share this path with us and to offer us his gaze so that we might see the light within it.

Encyclical Letter Lumen Fidei *to the Bishops, Priests, and Deacons Consecrated Persons and the Lay Faithful, on Faith, St. Peter's Square, June 29, 2013*

Time

In union with faith and charity, hope propels us toward a sure future, set against a different horizon with regard to the illusory enticements of the idols of this world, yet granting new momentum and strength to our daily lives. Let us refuse to be robbed of hope, or to allow our hope to be dimmed by facile answers and solutions, which block our progress, "fragmenting" time and changing it into space. Time is always much greater than space. Space hardens processes, whereas time propels toward the future and encourages us to go forward in hope.

Encyclical Letter Lumen Fidei *to the Bishops, Priests, and Deacons Consecrated Persons and the Lay Faithful, on Faith, St. Peter's Square, June 29, 2013*

Conscience

We must learn to listen to our conscience more. But be careful! This does not mean following my own ego, doing what interests me, what suits me, what I like. . . . It is not this! The conscience is the interior place for listening to the truth, to goodness, for listening to God; it is the inner place of my relationship with him, the One who speaks to my heart and helps me to discern, to understand the way I must take and, once the decision is made, to go forward, to stay faithful. We have had a marvelous example of what this relationship with God is like . . . Benedict XVI gave us this great example when the Lord made him understand, in prayer, what the step was that he had to take. With a great sense of discernment and courage, he followed his conscience; that is, the will of God speaking in his heart.

Angelus, *St. Peter's Square, June 30, 2013*

Encounter

True joy does not come from things or from possessing, no! It is born from the encounter, from the relationship with others, it is born from feeling accepted, understood, and loved, and from accepting, from understanding, and from loving; and this is not because of a passing fancy, but because the other is a person. Joy is born from the gratuitousness of an encounter! It is hearing someone say, but not necessarily with words, "You are important to me." This is beautiful. . . . And it is these very words that God makes us understand. In calling you God says to you, "You are important to me, I love you, I am counting on you." Jesus says this to each one of us! Joy is born from that! The joy of the moment in which Jesus looked at me. Understanding and hearing this is the secret of our joy. Feeling loved by God, feeling that for him we are not numbers but people, and hearing him calling us.

Meeting with Seminarians and Novices, Paul VI Audience Hall, July 6, 2013

———

Proclamation

The purpose is not to socialize, to spend time together; no, the purpose is to proclaim the Kingdom of God, and this is urgent! And it is still urgent today! There is no time to be lost in gossip, there is no need to wait for everyone's consensus; what is necessary is to go out and proclaim. To all people you bring the peace of Christ, and if they do not welcome it, you go ahead just the same. To the sick you bring healing, because God wants to heal man of every evil. How many missionaries do this—they sow life, health, comfort to the outskirts of the world. How beautiful it is! Do not live for yourselves, do not live for yourselves, but live to go forth and do good!

Angelus, *St. Peter's Square, July 7, 2013*

Indifference

We have lost a sense of responsibility for our brothers and sisters. We have fallen into the hypocrisy of the priest and the levite whom Jesus described in the parable of the Good Samaritan: we see our brother half-dead on the side of the road, and perhaps we say to ourselves, "Poor soul . . . !" and then go on our way. It's not our responsibility, and with that we feel reassured, assuaged. The culture of comfort, which makes us think only of ourselves, makes us insensitive to the cries of other people, makes us live in soap bubbles that, however lovely, are insubstantial; they offer a fleeting and empty illusion that results in indifference to others; indeed, it even leads to the globalization of indifference. In this globalized world, we have fallen into globalized indifference. We have become used to the suffering of others: it doesn't affect me. . . .

Visit to Lampedusa, "Arena" sports camp, Salina Quarter, July 8, 2013

Weeping

Has any one of us wept because of this situation and others like it? Has any one of us grieved for the death of these brothers and sisters? Has any one of us wept for these persons who were on the boat? For the young mothers carrying their babies? For these men who were looking for a means of supporting their families? We are a society that has forgotten how to weep, how to experience compassion—"suffering with" others: the globalization of indifference has taken from us the ability to weep!

Visit to Lampedusa, "Arena" sports camp, Salina Quarter, July 8, 2013

Values

I too come to knock on the door of the house of Mary—who loved and raised Jesus—that she may help all of us, pastors of God's people, parents and educators, to pass on to our young people the values that can help them build a nation and a world that are more just, united, and fraternal. For this reason I would like to speak of three simple attitudes: hopefulness, openness to being surprised by God, and living in joy.

Homily of the Holy Mass, Basilica of the Shrine of Our Lady of the Conception of Aparecida, Rio de Janeiro, July 24, 2013

To Embrace

We all have to learn to embrace the one in need, as St. Francis did. There are so many situations in Brazil, and throughout the world, that require attention, care, and love, like the fight against chemical dependency. Often, instead, it is selfishness that prevails in our society. How many "dealers of death" there are that follow the logic of power and money at any cost! The scourge of drug trafficking, which favors violence and sows the seeds of suffering and death, requires of society as a whole an act of courage. A reduction in the spread and influence of drug addiction will not be achieved by a liberalization of drug use, as is currently being proposed in various parts of Latin America. . . . We all need to look upon one another with the loving eyes of Christ, and to learn to embrace those in need, in order to show our closeness, affection, and love.

Address during the visit to St. Francis of Assisi of the Providence of God Hospital-VOT,
Rio de Janeiro, July 24, 2013

Young People

You young people, my dear young friends, you have a particular sensitivity toward injustice, but you are often disappointed by facts that speak of corruption on the part of people who put their own interests before the common good. To you and to all, I repeat: never yield to discouragement, do not lose trust, do not allow your hope to be extinguished. Situations can change, people can change. Be the first to seek to bring good, do not grow accustomed to evil, but defeat it with good. The Church is with you, bringing you the precious good of faith, bringing Jesus Christ, who "came that they may have life and have it abundantly."

Visit to the Community of Varginha (Manginhos), Rio de Janeiro, July 25, 2013

Prayer to Mary

Mother, help our faith! Open our ears to hear God's word and to recognize his voice and call. Awaken in us a desire to follow in his footsteps, to go forth from our own land, and to receive his promise. Help us to be touched by his love, that we may touch him in faith. Help us to entrust ourselves fully to him and to believe in his love, especially at times of trial, beneath the shadow of the cross, when our faith is called to mature. Sow in our faith the joy of the Risen One. Remind us that those who believe are never alone. Teach us to see all things with the eyes of Jesus, that he may be light for our path. And may this light of faith always increase in us, until the dawn of that undying day, which is Christ himself, your Son, our Lord!

Encyclical Letter Lumen Fidei *to the Bishops, Priests, and Deacons Consecrated Persons and the Lay Faithful, on Faith, St. Peter's Square, June 29, 2013*

Index

First published in the United States of America in 2014 by
Rizzoli International Publications, Inc.
300 Park Avenue South
New York, NY 10010
www.rizzoliusa.com

Originally published in Italian as *Francesco: Uno di Noi* in 2013 by
RCS Libri S.p.A.

Photographs © "L'Osservatore Romano" Photographic Service
except the following:
© Andrew Medichini/AP Photo/Lapresse, p. 35
© Gregorio Borgia/AP Photo/Lapresse, p. 46
© AP Photo/Lapresse, p. 65
© Alessandra Tarantino/AP Photo/Lapresse, pp. 203, 224–225, 239
© Victor R. Caivano/AP Photo/Lapresse, p. 258
© Felipe Dana/AP Photo/Lapresse, pp. 260–261
© Archivio Shutterstock, pp. 14, 90, 151
Courtesy Gianluca Castagna, p. 196

Texts © 2013 The Vatican Publishing House, Vatican City
The publisher has made every effort to identify the copyright holders.

Introduction by Vincenzo Sansonetti, translated by Sheila Beatty
Art direction and layout by Ultreya, Milan

2014 2015 2016 2017 / 10 9 8 7 6 5 4 3 2 1

ISBN: 978-0-8478-4553-8

Library of Congress Control Number: 2014942439

Printed in China